NEWPORT
TENNESSEE

NEWPORT
TENNESSEE
Pictures from the Past

Edward R. Walker III

THE
History
PRESS

Published by The History Press
Charleston, SC 29403
www.historypress.net

Copyright © 2010 by Edward Walker
All rights reserved

Front cover, top, courtesy Sally M. Burnett.
Front cover, bottom, from the author's collection.
First published 2010

Manufactured in the United States

ISBN 978.1.59629.927.6

Walker, Edward R., 1950-
Newport, Tennessee : pictures from the past / Edward Walker.
p. cm.
ISBN 978-1-59629-927-6
1. Newport (Tenn.)--History--Pictorial works. 2. Newport (Tenn.)--Social life and customs--Pictorial works. I. Title.
F444.N48W35 2010
976.8'895--dc22
2010018560

Notice: The information in this book is true and complete to the best of our knowledge. It is offered without guarantee on the part of the author or The History Press. The author and The History Press disclaim all liability in connection with the use of this book.

All rights reserved. No part of this book may be reproduced or transmitted in any form whatsoever without prior written permission from the publisher except in the case of brief quotations embodied in critical articles and reviews.

Contents

Acknowledgements	7
Introduction	9
Citizens	13
Homes	35
Business/Industry	47
Education	67
Scenes	77
Transportation	89
Civic Organizations	103
Religions	125
Recreation	137
Appendix: Group Photograph Identifications	153
About the Author	159

Acknowledgements

The real appreciation for this work is due to the photographers, most of them unknown, who made the pictures found herein. Some of them were professionals and others amateurs, but all had that talent common to photographers. Some of those persons did this photography as their sole vocations while others did it in conjunction with their jobs. There were some who just happened to have a camera in hand when the opportunity to capture a scene, a moment in time, occurred.

A number of these photographs were newspaper glossy prints that had been collected by Ethel Sweeten McCoig. In pre-computer days, newspapers used photographs that had been taken with film that had to be developed. Often, several prints of the same event were made. After their use in an issue, these prints were stored until a need for space necessitated their disposal. At such times, Nancy Petrey of the *Newport Plain Talk* passed them on to Mrs. McCoig. After McCoig's death, the collection was passed on to Duay O'Neil, who has willingly shared them.

Chris Edmonds is another local citizen who has a passion for collecting and preserving the community's history. The amount of local memorabilia that he has collected is astounding—pictures, yes, but many other items such as posters, calendars, invoices, receipts, pencils, tickets and advertisements. For most people, these items would be considered junk, but Chris views each of them as a glimpse into the community's past. He, too, has been most generous in making these available.

There are others who shared pictures and time when contacted about a picture, an identification or a clarification. This is also appreciated.

Acknowledgements

To everyone, a word of advice: please identify your pictures. It is amazing how quickly names are lost, and persons once significant in our community and our lives become nameless faces in a photograph.

Then, as always, there are Cindy and Claire, the most important people in my life, who are tolerant and understanding of my interest in "that old stuff."

Thanks to you all!

Introduction

This is a photographic history of Newport, Tennessee, the county seat of Cocke County, basically pre-1980. Earlier, similar photographic collections have been published, and it has been a goal of this project to use photographs that have not been published in any of the other collections. It is in no way an all-inclusive work, nor is it a terminal one. The surface has just been scratched. All around this area on bookshelves and in albums, closets and dresser drawers are many glimpses of local history just waiting to tell their own stories.

The familiar phrase "A picture's worth a thousand words" supposedly first appeared in a trade journal in 1921, even though a similar remark was attributed to Napoleon Bonaparte. There truly is so much that can be learned from pictures that have captured persons and scenes exactly as they were at a particular moment. As historians work to uncover and preserve the past, photographs have been a valuable resource.

Although modern photography originated in France, historians have found evidence of experimentation with photographic principles in ancient Greece and China. Joseph Nicéphore Niépce of France made the first still-life photograph in 1826, but after his death in 1833, his partner Louis Daguerre perfected the process, which became known as the "daguerreotype," where an image is transferred to a chemically treated copper surface. This concept soon reached the United States.

Over the years, research continued, and images increasingly could be reproduced on other surfaces, such as glass, iron and paper. The first photographs were costly and were only available in the metropolitan areas and within the reach of the wealthy. As costs decreased, photographs

Introduction

became more affordable to the general public, but even then, the "shooting" of photographs required the skillful use of expensive equipment.

After the Civil War, photographic studios began to be established in smaller cities and towns, just as traveling photographers began plying their trade throughout the country, particularly at public gatherings such as county fairs. Their "tintypes" (actually thin sheets of iron) were sometimes called "penny pictures" because of their minimal cost. Some photographers went from house to house, and often the entire family would pose with a pretty quilt as a backdrop.

One local photographer was John S. Bushong, a Virginian who married a local girl, Mary Harned. In the 1870s, Bushong's family was listed in Parrottsville, but he was working in Athens, Tennessee.

In 1972, an elderly relative of Mrs. Bushong recalled, "People came to his studio to have their pictures made. Sometimes he loaded up his studio on a wagon and traveled from one community to another taking pictures."

The photograph of a Newport woman bearing Bushong's label is evidence that he was here during his professional career. Other early photographers were Aaron Bible in Del Rio, Jonas Canupp on Cosby and J.A. Breeden in Bybee.

There are only a minimal number of existing local photographs before 1880. After that, more are extant, but portraits and groups seem to have been made rather than scenes, possibly because of the expense involved and the limited market for such pictures. Sadly, many of the early photographs are unidentified.

Newport's first resident photographer was J.H. Fagala, whose shop was on the northwest corner of Main Street and Court Avenue on the site long occupied by the Newport Laundry. Fagala was here in 1880, but he does not list his occupation as "photographer" until 1910, even though the 1887 Sanborn Fire Insurance map shows a photography shop on the site. Mrs. Mims wrote this about him in a newspaper article in the *Newport Times* in 1940:

> *The little photograph building and tinshop stood in the corner of the yard. Many a schoolgirl was delighted with a tintype picture of her best chum with all decked out in tiebacks and bangs…About the year 1884 Mr. Fagala erected a two story building on the corner…and moved his photographic studio to the upper floor…He was really a good photographer for his day. He may not have used all of the modern tricks of posture and composition, but I now have specimens of his work more than forty years old, quite fresh and unfaded.*

Introduction

Fagala occasionally must have had some competition, for a newspaper item in 1894 noted that photographer J.M. Honey of Morristown had set up his "neat portable house" and was available to take pictures "opposite the Click House" (which now houses the Newport Police Department). In a subsequent issue, it was reported that Honey had moved on and had taken his "neat little house" (described then as a tent) with him.

Mention should be made of another part of Newport's photographic history. The picture postcard became popular in America in the early 1900s, and John Glenn, the owner of a variety store in downtown Newport, marketed a line of postcards featuring scenes about town. These are some of the earliest local scenes, although the name of the actual photographer is unknown.

George Eastman developed flexible, paper-based film to replace photographic plates in 1884. He patented the film roll camera in 1889. Reverend Hannibal Goodwin patented celluloid film in 1898. All of these innovations led to the 1900 introduction of Eastman's Brownie cardboard camera, which cost one dollar (about twenty-five dollars in today's currency). By the next year, Eastman determined that the cameras would have to be made of sturdier material. Most users returned their film to the dealer for processing, but a "developing outfit" was offered by Eastman for seventy-five cents. It is a bit startling to realize that this little invention was part of the communication pathway, just like photojournalism and the Internet of today.

Although probably available much earlier, by 1911 Smith Drug Store was advertising in the *Newport Plain Talk* that it had Kodak Brownie's for seven dollars, as well as photographic supplies, printing frames, enlarging cameras, developing services and, no doubt, the little black albums in which to mount all of the photographs that were made.

The Brownie put photography into the hands of the general public, and after 1900, more and more pictures, often called "kodaks," were made. The people who had a Brownie thought that they were only dealing with the present and had little idea that they were recording history. The faces, scenes, buildings and events that they photographed were captured for posterity. There have always been those with a pronounced interest in photography and who always seemed to have a camera at hand. In 1948, the local newspaper made mention of citizens such as Clay Overholt, Mulford Lillard, Jim Wood, Shell Clevenger, Gray O'Neil, Frank Gorman, Ben D. Stokely and Asa Wilson, all of whom had gotten into the 8mm home movie craze.

Introduction

When asked about "old pictures," many people mistakenly believe that only those made by a professional photographer have any historical value. Not so! In a way, everyday photographs, the kodaks, can tell a much broader story, not only of their primary subjects but also of the backgrounds. As each year passes, the snapshots become more precious, reminiscent of persons and events passed. There is scarcely a home that does not possess at least one "favorite" photograph.

Other than Fagala, Newport has had other professional photographers. Mamye Campbell, who died in 1943, had a photograph shop and an ice cream parlor where the Men's Den is now located. Just up the street was Nina's Photo Shoppe, where film was developed and enlargements made. (Sadly, as of 2010, no one can recall Nina's last name.) Coincidentally, Elza Painter did photography work for over forty years on the same block. Located first on McMahan Avenue in 1959, he later moved around the corner to 230 East Broadway. Although she did not do such work for a living, Mrs. Charles Rhyne Sr. had advanced equipment both for still photographs and 16mm movies. One of her photographs of the German prisoners of war in Hot Springs even appeared in the *New York Times* in 1918.

Today's cameras are both more efficient and proficient, taking photographs is easier, processing them is quicker and the love of photographs remains strong. If there could be one change, I would have that anyone taking photographs do so with a sense that history is being recorded.

Those photographs with the designation of "NPT" are from the *Newport Plain Talk*. SML refers to Stokely Memorial Library. An asterisk (*) will indicate those group photographs whose identifications are found in the appendix. Although every effort was made to secure identifications, some persons in the pictures could not be identified.

May the photographs shown here evoke good memories of the people and places that are a part of your past.

CITIZENS

Whatever makes men good Christians, makes them good citizens.
—Daniel Webster (1782–1852)

While buildings and houses are important, it is the people who really make a community. Every town has a variety of citizens, each one with unique characteristics—some more positive than others. It takes this variety to construct the fabric and personality of a place.

Coming after the Native Americans, the first permanent white citizen here was John Gilliland, who had a crop of corn at the forks of the Big Pigeon and French Broad Rivers in 1781, although it was supposedly 1783 before he brought his family here. Gilliland received his grant for service in the American Revolution. His son, John Jr., donated the fifty acres in 1799 to establish a county seat for the new Cocke County.

Today, more than two centuries later, Gilliland descendants are still here.

Newport has never been a large town, but there has been growth. Some population counts have included 345 in 1880; 900 in 1887; 1,000 in 1892; 1,500 in 1903; 2,000 in 1913; 3,200 in 1930; 3,575 in 1940; 3,892 in 1950; 6,448 in 1960; 7,328 in 1970; 7,580 in 1980; and 7,123 in 1990. The population for 2009 was estimated to be 7,449.

Citizens are, and have always been, human beings first. Our ancestors were subject to the same basic strengths and weakness that are found in society today. It is hard to imagine that these people who faced so many obstacles when establishing a new community in the wilderness could be anything but perfect. Read the early church minutes and learn what foibles were exhibited by those early folks!

Too often, only a small percentage of the citizenry is recognized in history for its role in building the community, the state and the nation. It takes all kinds of folks to do this: the movers and shakers; management and labor; those who abide by the law and those who don't; the young and the old; the beautiful and the not so beautiful; and the haves and the have-nots. How dull it would be if everything in life was the same.

Larger surrounding communities have tended to denigrate the citizens of Newport and Cocke County based on the actions of a few, but anyone who chooses to look beyond this minority of people and the bad publicity will find caring people who will go over and beyond to help one another. Yes, there are areas that could use improvement, but what town doesn't have those?

The pictures included here are only a representative sample of the folks who have made Newport what it is and has been. Certainly, the persons in these pictures were not all equal in their accomplishments or contributions to the community, but they all played a role. Would that a volume could be published with a picture of each and every citizen!

Mrs. Anna Stokely, pictured with her family. She and her sons founded the canning industry that has meant so much to Newport. *Sally M. Burnett.* *

Pictures from the Past

Above: The Fisher family came here in 1892 to establish the Unaka Tannery. This picture was made about 1897. *SML Collection.* *

Right: County Surveyor C.B. McNabb is shown in front of his office on the southwest corner of Woodlawn and Mulberry. McNabb did the original plat for Union Cemetery in 1898. *McNabb Collection.*

Newport, Tennessee

Left: Attorney W.J. McSween (1848–1914) was well known in the region for his pugnacious approach to the cases he handled and the causes he espoused. He was the first person to make a serious attempt to preserve the local history when he first penned his "Recollections of Newport and Cocke County" in 1903. *Roger Branson.*

Below: Dr. Boonlua Lucktong, a native of Thailand, practiced medicine here in the 1980s. *NPT photo.*

Pictures from the Past

Four generations of the family of Sarah Margery Murphy O'Brien (1834–1916) are pictured here. Mrs. O'Brien was born in Stratford-on-Avon, England, and moved to Cocke County about 1872. After her husband died, she supported her family by teaching school here. *McNabb Collection.* *

Thomas Sandusky Gorman (1812–1876) has sometimes been called "the father of Newport" because of his role in establishing the "new" Newport on the Big Pigeon River. He donated the land for the depot, the courthouse and the Masonic Hall. *Author's collection.*

Vote for
William M. Crawford
Candidate for Congress

[Over]

Above: City Recorder Gene Layman (far right) and Alderman Reece Balch (far left) swear in the reserve police officers in 1975. *NPT photo.* *

Left: W.M. Crawford (1889–1956) was a longtime attorney in Newport. *Author's collection.*

Pictures from the Past

Above: Cocke County Memorial Hospital, a Hill-Burton facility, opened in 1970. Director of Nurses Marion Roberts (standing) consults with nurses Peggy West (left) and Brenda Hall (right). The facility is now Baptist Hospital. *NPT photo.*

Right: Cleo Balch of Maloy Funeral Home is shown raking leaves in front of the funeral home. *NPT photo.*

Newport, Tennessee

For many years, Mrs. Cora Brown and her son, Tip, owned and operated Brown Funeral Home, which had been established in 1930 by Tip Brown Sr. *NPT photo.*

Y.J. McMahan (1861–1939) was associated with Merchants and Planters Bank for over fifty years. The fact that at least a dozen boys were named for him attests to his popularity. *Beverly C. Little.*

Pictures from the Past

Above: Colonel Dewey Strange (right) was active in local affairs for many years—in the county court, farming community, Cocke County Fair and his church. *NPT photo*.

Right: Starting with just a few pieces of used furniture in 1926, T.E. Freeman established a business that has been a part of Newport for seventy years. *Rolan Freeman*.

21

NEWPORT, TENNESSEE

This 1952 photo illustrates the strong Republican sentiment in the community. Oscar Gregg, a Democrat, looks at the additions that have been added to his Stevenson poster. *O.P. Gregg.*

Officer Ed Stuart and meter maid Frances Clevenger direct traffic on Woodlawn Avenue in 1971. *NPT photo.*

Pictures from the Past

Right: A community activist for many years, Joe Bacon made both friends and enemies with his views on local politics. *NPT photo.*

Below: Jack-of-all-trades Jim Dunn also authored columns in the local newspapers from time to time. *NPT photo.*

Newport, Tennessee

With no business experience, Mrs. Emma Stokely established a successful insurance business after her husband's death in 1929. She sold her business in 1972 at the age of eighty-four. *NPT photo.*

Reverend S.E. Loxley (1884–1986) served as pastor of Second Baptist Church and later operated a local credit bureau. As a boy growing up in Dayton, Ohio, he knew the Wright brothers, who had the first manned air flight. *NPT photo.*

Pictures from the Past

Ben Bynum, an herb doctor, is pictured on Main Street in 1908. He died in 1915. *Burnett Smith Collection.*

W. Riley Neas (1873–1963) owned and operated a farm supply store, W.R. Neas and Company, on Broadway on the present National Bank of Tennessee site. *NPT photo.*

Newport, Tennessee

Above: J. Glenn ("Jug") Ramsey will be remembered both for his line work with Newport Utilities and his love of fox hunting. *NPT photo.*

Left: Lois Reese was affiliated with C.D. Fisher Insurance for over fifty years. Pictured with her are Judge J. Kenneth Porter and Ronald Bullard. *NPT photo.*

Pictures from the Past

The McSween brothers—Sam, George, Lome and Burl—posed together in 1915. Lome was a mayor of Newport, George was employed by the T&NC Railroad and Sam had a store in Eastport. *Author's collection.*

Representing the First Congressional District, 1963–97, James H. "Jimmy" Quillen was beloved in Cocke County. He is shown speaking at the Cocke County Courthouse in the early days of his term. *NPT photo.*

W. Hugh Huff was an early insurance agent in Newport, as well as a staunch Southern Methodist. *Author's collection.*

A.A. Arthur came here in 1884 with the Scottish-Carolina Timber and Land Company, which startled little Newport with its influx of persons from many different locales. Due to a lack of cooperation among local leaders, both Arthur and the SCTL left here in 1886. *Author's collection.*

Pictures from the Past

Eva Babb Sexton was a great booster for Newport. For many years, she was with the chamber of commerce. Later employed by the city, she oversaw many beautification projects around town: street planters, the dogwood grove, Newport City Park gardens, the local history park and Pisgah Presbyterian Cemetery. *Doris N. Teague.*

Although her career was in home economics, Mary Rowe Ruble, as county historian, began the genealogical collection at Stokely Memorial Library. *SML Collection.*

C.L. Goughnour came to Newport in 1913 and established an electrical power operation from a dam on Big Pigeon River below Waterville. *Author's collection.*

In his role as Santa Claus, Mack Leibrock delighted many children at Christmas. Not only was he employed by businesses, but families often arranged his appearance on Christmas Eve. *Wilma Davies.*

Pictures from the Past

Right: The Newport Fire Department has conducted the Toys for Tots campaign at Christmas for many years. Chief Roger Butler (center) is shown with Alderman Harold Allen (right) and Mike Hill of Sammons Communication. *NPT photo.*

Below: R.P. Sulte (left) purchased the *Newport Plain Talk* from Tom Campbell in 1926. *Clyde Driskill Jr.*

31

J.L. Caton edited both the *Newport Times* and the *Newport Plain Talk*. Author's collection.

Arthur Petrey came to the *Newport Plain Talk* from the *Elizabethton Star* in 1959. *NPT photo.*

Pictures from the Past

After her husband's death in 1981, Nancy Petrey assumed the management of the paper. *NPT photo.*

Present editor David Popiel began work at the newspaper in 1973. *NPT photo.*

Above Left: Charles B. Mims (1859–1938) served as mayor of Newport, as well as operated the Mims Store and the Mims Hotel. *Sally M. Burnett.*

Above Right: Alex Buda, a native of Albania, came to Newport and opened the Busy Bee Café at the intersection of Broadway and McMahan. Shown with him is his grandson, Billy. *Janice Casey.*

Below: Newport mayor and aldermen are sworn in on January 1, 1965. *Roy T. Campbell Jr.* *

HOMES

Go where he will, the wise man is at home.
—Ralph Waldo Emerson (1803–1882)

Home and hearth have long been glorified in both poetry and prose. Protection from the elements of nature is one of the basics of life, and a home will provide that whether it is a humble hut or a magnificent mansion. Where there are people, there are homes.

The scarcity of early records limits what is known about the first residents here. W.J. McSween's "Recollections of Newport and Cocke County," a newspaper series first published in 1903, reports that the first county court was held on November 27, 1797, at the home of Daniel Adams, which was located approximately on the present site of Goodwill Industries. If there were other residents in the location then, it's unknown.

Another early home in what is now Newport was that of the Sandusky family that stood on the site of the Memorial Building. Emanuel Sandusky received a grant for ninety-seven acres along the river in 1809. By the time of the Civil War, most of that land was still in the hands of the Gormans, grandchildren of Sandusky. According to W.W. Langhorne, when he arrived here in 1867, there were only two *substantial* houses. The David H. Gorman house was a frame structure located about where A&W/Long John Silver is now, and the Thomas S. Gorman house was brick and was located three-fourths of a mile east on the present Beauty Box site.

The oldest house now standing in the environs of Newport, and possibly the entire county, is "Beechwood Hall," which was built about 1804 by William Garrett; it is now the home of the Graham family. A close second would be the Gilliland-O'Dell house in Oldtown, which carries the date of 1814.

As the present community progressed from Clifton to Gorman's Depot to Newport, with the arrival of the railroad and the removal of the county seat, more people began moving into the area and more homes were built. The business district was on Main Street mainly from Woodlawn to McSween; east and west of that was residential. There were at least thirty homes on Main Street along the tracks, which attested to the desirability of that location. Today, only four of those old homes remain, though they are greatly modified for business: Costner-Maloy Funeral Home, Newport Police Department, Brown Funeral Home and Manes Funeral Home. However, many citizens can recall some of the others.

Residential areas began springing up in other places. With the arrival of the Scottish Company, families moved eastward, though still along the river and the railroad. Then, homes began being built up in what was officially the "Jones-Randolph Addition" but is now just known as "Jones Hill." With a bridge across the river by 1881, Clifton Heights and Northport developed. The Newport Development Company sold off lots in 1890 in the area now called "Eastport." In the early 1900s, West End became home to more citizens.

The boundaries of Newport have expanded in all directions—and home construction with it. Edgar A. Guest said, "It takes a' heap of livin' to make a house a home." That's just what happens within the walls of a house. Within the ones pictured here, and those that aren't, there are stories of families, their lives and their experiences.

Pictures from the Past

Greenlawn was built by General Alexander Smith, a Revolutionary soldier. Later, it was the home of his only son, Alexander Evans Smith. It stood a short distance west of River Rest Apartments. It was razed about 1985. *SML Collection.*

This house was built about 1814 by Abel Gilliland, son of the first settler, John Gilliland. Later, it belonged to the Camerons, but for over 125 years it has been home to the O'Dell family. It is the only remnant of old Newport. *SML Collection.*

Thomas S. Gorman built this house about 1845. In 1876, it was sold to William McSween, whose family still owned it until shortly before it burned down in 1963. *SML Collection.*

Mrs. Emily Swanson and her daughters, Ollie and Bert, are shown in front of their boardinghouse, which was located on Broadway on the site now occupied by attorneys Whitson and Moore. *Author's collection.*

Pictures from the Past

The R.P. Driskill home was located on the southwest corner of Church and C Streets. It was razed in 1968, and the Newport Fire Department now occupies the site. *Sally M. Burnett.*

W.J. McSween built this home in 1876 on East Main Street. The family resided here until 1960, when the property was sold and razed. Food City now occupies the site. *Roger Branson.*

Located on the corner of North and Smith Streets, the Robert L. Talley home was built about 1900. In later years, the porch was enlarged. Shown here in 1903 are Mrs. Talley; her daughters Elna, Mary Moore and Bonnie Kate; and her sister Edna Huff. This is now the home of Craig Ward and family. *Ann Ward.*

C.L. Goughnour built this bungalow, ultramodern for 1914, from which he could control the electrical current generated from his dam, some eighteen miles upriver. The house also featured a primitive air conditioning system. It is now the property of Iliff McMahan Jr. *Author's collection.*

Pictures from the Past

The Y.J. McMahan home was located on West Broadway on the present Sonic site. After the McMahans died, it was the home of their daughter, Mrs. J.O. Cope, and her family. *Beverly C. Little.*

The original portion of the Masters home at 543 Fifth Street was built by F.S. Graddon about 1897. Mr. and Mrs. Herbert Masters purchased the home in 1927. Their son, James P. Masters, remodeled it to its present appearance. *James P. Masters.*

The office of C.B. McNabb was on the corner of Woodlawn and Mulberry. To the rear was his home. Later, his son, C.C. McNabb, built his home on the site of the office. *McNabb Collection.*

Pictures from the Past

It was in the older portion of the William Vinson home that Pleasant Grove Baptist Church was organized in 1838. This portion, shown here, was added about 1890. This rendition in needlepoint was done by Betty Vinson Lenderman. *Adeline S. Foster.*

The George F. Smith home was built in 1894. Originally, the front lawn went all the way to Woodlawn Avenue. In 1930, a miniature golf course was established on the site. This is now the home of the Watts family. *Burnett Smith Collection.*

The Scottish Mansion was built in 1885 to showcase the various varieties of lumber produced by the company. About 1900 it became the home of the Anderson family. The house burned down in 1975. *Author's collection.*

Pictures from the Past

The home of J.S. and Nannie Allen stood on the southeast corner of West Main Street and Jefferson Avenue, just across from the mill. *Alexander Collection.*

This picture is an early view of River Road. The row of houses on the upper side of the street was owned by J.R. Seehorn and descendants, and those on the lower side, by L.S. Smith and descendants. The large building in the background was the Bellevue Cotton Mill, located near the railroad underpass. The present site of Riverview Baptist Church would be on the far right of the photo. *Chris Edmonds.*

The Harrison Sexton home was on East Main Street, on the site now occupied by the parking lot for the courthouse annex. This picture is dated 1922. In later years, this was the home of the Oscar O'Neil family. *Mrs. W.C. Vinson.*

Business/Industry

Man goeth forth unto his work and to his labour...
—Psalms 104:23

Why do men and women work? There could be more than one answer to that question, but the fact remains that work is a necessity and has been since the very beginning. Adam himself had this responsibility when God charged him to "keep and dress" the Garden of Eden. Still later, when Adam and Eve were banished from the garden, the Lord decreed that from then forward man would have to earn his bread by the sweat of his brow.

While this country primarily once had an agricultural economy, in which citizens were self-sufficient of their farms, there were always those other persons whose talents furnished goods and services that the farmers could not always produce. In the ensuing years, the farm is no longer the sole source of income for most citizens, even though there are many who still have not totally severed their ties to the land, as is evidenced by those who still maintain vegetable gardens.

In the 1870 census for Newport and its environs, some citizens listed "farmer" or "farm laborer" as occupations, but also listed were such occupations as blacksmith, miller, merchant, carpenter, physician, tailor, clerk, shoemaker, domestic servant, barber, lawyer, grocer, brick mason, minister, seamstress and all the ladies who were keeping house. In 1880 in Newport, there were even fewer farmers listed, and in addition to the above occupations, there were occupations like wheelwright, cabinetmaker, jeweler, hotel keeper, druggist, barkeeper, tanner, dentist, livestock dealer, painter, tinner, teacher, bridge builder, printer, washwoman, editor and clock tinkerer.

Newport, Tennessee

Even when women generally toiled in the home, in early Newport there were those women who had occupations outside of the home. Mrs. Mims recalled how Mrs. Mattie Peterson did most of the work in her husband's store, which also held the Newport post office. Mrs. Emily Swanson operated the first eating establishment here. Mrs. Ben Jones had a bonnet shop, and Miss Sallie Anderson sold books and stationery. With women such as these, the pathway to wider vocational opportunities for women began.

The first store in present-day Newport was that of Thomas Evans on the site of Wilson SavMor Drugs. Following soon after were the businesses by C.T. Peterson, Edward Clark, Roadman and Gorman and John M. Jones.

The first manufacturing operation would have been the Gorman mill on Big Pigeon River, which was purchased by the Randolphs in 1871. The mill ground flour and meal, as well as sawed and planed lumber. The Scottish-Carolina Timber and Land Company operated here from 1884 to 1886. After it departed, the Newport Development Company worked to bring industry into town. One of its most successful attempts was the Unaka Tannery that operated from 1893 until 1976.

Just as Newport's population has increased, so have its job opportunities, as well as the overall standard of living.

For over 115 years, a pharmacy has been located on the corner of Broadway and McMahan. In 1893, George F. Smith opened Smith Drug Store. This photo shows the interior in 1912. About 1935, Lyde Stokely and Judson Shults purchased the business. About 1983, Wilson-SavMor moved to the site. *Burnett Smith Collection.*

Pictures from the Past

Above: This was the Jones store on West Main Street in 1902. It is now a warehouse for Freeman's Furniture. *Alexander Collection.*

Right: The Pet Milk processing plant is shown here in 1961. When this operation closed, the company donated the property to the city, and now the site is the Pet Milk Playground. *Author's collection.*

Seehorn Hardware Co.
QUALITY HARDWARE

Left: Seehorn Hardware was first located on Main Street. Later it was moved to this building on McMahan Avenue. The building was razed in 1996. *Author's collection.*

Below: The W.B. Robinson warehouse was located diagonally across from Smith Drug Store. The site is now part of North Street. *Burnett Smith Collection.*

Pictures from the Past

PAPER, TIN and WASTE FATS

ARE more urgently needed than at any time during this war. Save and bring in your waste paper, prepared tin cans and waste fats. Newport's Paper Depot is at J. W. Rice's Coal Yard on Cosby Cut-Off. The following grocery stores have agreed to accept Waste FATS and PREPARED TIN CANS:

B. & H. GROCERY	WHITE STORE	BROADWAY FOOD MARKET
J. C. HENRY	THRIFT MARKET	FRED CAMPBELL
A & P TEA COMPANY	L & F GROCERY	HAWK GROCERY
CASH MEAT MARKET	BRYANT GROCERY	
MAURICE SUGGS GROCERY	M. L. MANTOOTH	CARL SUTTON'S GROCERY

This is a county-wide drive and schools are co-operating. Any grocer not having an outlet for waste fats may take it to Mr. Wells, White store, who has agreed to handle it. This is your war as well as the fighting man's. Don't fail to do your part. We shipped one car load of waste paper in January of 41,050 pounds, and have been asked to ship two car loads in February.

E. R. WALKER, Chairman

This advertisement appeared in the *Newport Plain Talk* on January 29, 1945, and shows the work of local businesses in the war effort. *Author's collection.*

The Newport Federal Savings and Loan was organized in 1934. It became Newport Federal Bank in 1998. The employees are gathered here for their Christmas party in 1974 at their new building. *NPT photo.* *

Newport, Tennessee

Above: Holder Funeral Home was established in 1917 by John Holder. The business moved to this location, originally the H.H. Baer home, in 1937. In 1963, the business became Griffey Mortuary and later moved to another location. This site is now used for parking by Manes Funeral Home. *SML Collection.*

Left: John Holder got his start in the funeral business by driving a hearse for J.P. Hedrick, who rented a matched pair of horses from John's father, C.C. Holder, owner of a livery stable. *NPT photo.*

Pictures from the Past

N.L. McSween Hardware was located on the southeast corner of Woodlawn and Broadway. When this building burned down in 1965, it was occupied by Freeman's Furniture. *Chris Edmonds.*

Opened in 1920, Barnett and Bales Drug Store in 1922 became Nelson-Bales, which closed in 1973. The site is now used for National Bank of Tennessee parking. *Chris Edmonds.*

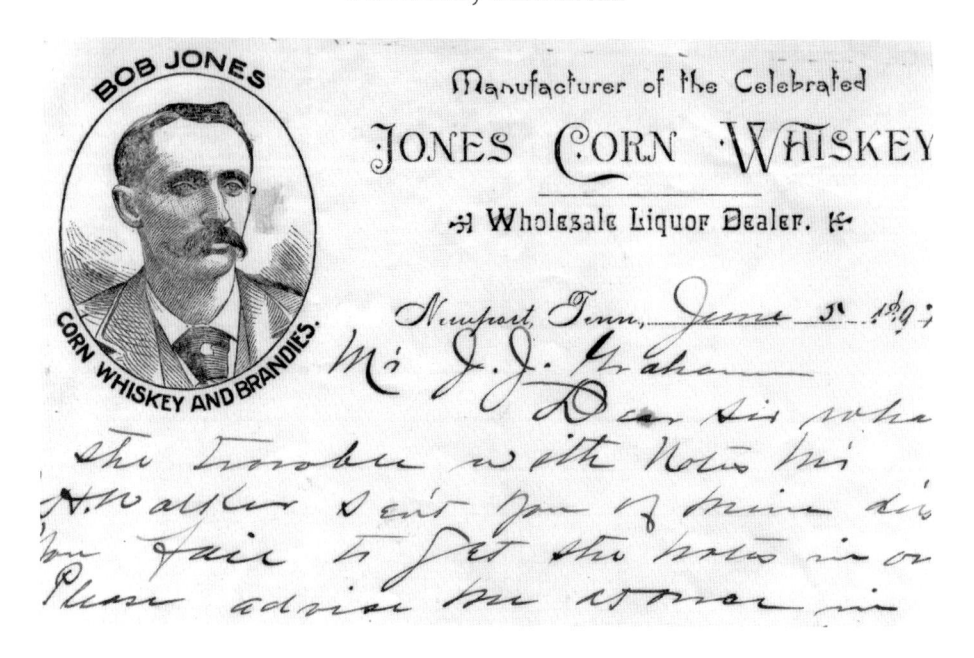

Above: The story of the production of illegal liquor is very familiar to local citizens, but Bob Jones had one of the legal distilleries. This is Jones's letterhead in 1897. *Chris Edmonds.*

Left: Rebecca F. Glenn, pictured in 1948, changed the name of her business to Glenn's Furniture. In 1965, she merged into Freeman's Furniture with her sons. *Rolan Freeman.*

Pictures from the Past

In 1931, White Store was one of the first chain groceries to locate in Newport. Its first location was on Main Street. Later it moved to 150 West Broadway and then, in 1964, to the Eastern Plaza Center. *NPT photo.* *

Jefferson-Cocke Utility District brought natural gas to the area in 1960. Pictured here in 1972 are directors M.M. Bullard, J.W. Ellis and C.D. Fisher and manager Tommy Young. *NPT photo.*

Clark Shoe Shop on McMahan Avenue handled shoe repairs for local citizens. Trained by his father, O.L. Clark Jr. is shown in 1974 putting on a heel. *NPT photo.*

Parks-Belk came to Newport in 1937. After the business burned down in 1962, it moved in 1964 to its new location, which closed in 1995. The building is now Manes Funeral Home. In 1975, employees Phil Owens and Elizabeth Bandy display a quilt made by Mrs. Bess Wilde, who is seated. *NPT photo.*

Pictures from the Past

George Miller Jr.'s career in used furniture began in 1946 but eventually evolved into an auction company that handled the sale of fine antiques and collectibles. *NPT photo.*

This photo, dated 1905, shows the Newport Post Office on Mims Avenue (now the U.S. Bank site). *Chris Edmonds.*

A modern post office was built in 1937 and was used until the operation moved to Cosby Highway in 1977. *Chris Edmonds.*

A group of postal employees gathered in 1972 to commemorate the retirement of several employees. *NPT photo.* *

Pictures from the Past

Above: The Newport Stock Market was located near the intersection of Cosby Highway and Old Cosby Road. Weekly sales were held here until 1973. *NPT photo.*

Right: For more than forty years, Ceton L. Lewis was involved in retail sales in downtown Newport as an employee, a partner and an owner. *Betty Jean Freeman.*

The Area Resource Center was a reference service of the Nolichucky Regional Library System. It was introduced to local businesses at a luncheon in 1971. *NPT photo.* *

This building, located at Bridgeport, was owned by Major James T. Huff, who is pictured at the right. His daughter, Elizabeth (shown at the left), managed the post office. R.H. Sexton had a store in the building. There were living quarters located upstairs. The building was razed in 1978. *Chris Edmonds.*

Pictures from the Past

The Department of Human Services staff is pictured here in 1972. *NPT photo.* *

First National Bank, organized in 1907, was located in 1910 in the building now occupied by Crown Credit. In 1917, it moved to a new building adjacent to First Baptist Church but fell victim to the Depression and closed in 1930. In this picture, the corner building, long occupied by Minnis Drugs, was the site of the New York Store, which sold clothing. *Chris Edmonds.*

Newport, Tennessee

Merchants and Planters Bank was established in 1889. In 1908, it moved to a new building on the southeast corner of Mims Avenue and East Main Street. A bank has been on this site ever since. This building was used until 1990. The original sign is outside the U.S. Bank. The bank employees standing in the door about 1912, *from left*, are Y.J. McMahan, John M. Jones, Elizabeth Stokely and Carl Mims. *Beverly C. Little.*

Shown here are the members of the original board of directors for National Bank of Newport (now National Bank of Tennessee), which opened for business in 1958. *Clyde Driskill Jr.**

Pictures from the Past

Using the power of the river, a mill was established on this site by the Gormans in the 1860s. The earliest portion of this building was erected about 1885 by Judge Randolph. Over the years, the ownership varied. The buildings were removed in 2003. *NPT photo.*

The mill office and warehouse is shown in 1902. *Alexander Collection.*

Pictures from the Past

The City Milling Company, located at the intersection of Cosby Highway and Broadway, was established about 1915. Burnett Produce last occupied the building, which was razed about 1974. *NPT photo.*

This Super Dollar Market was Newport's first modern, freestanding supermarket. This building was erected in 1955. Note the old McSween home in the rear. *Author's collection.*

Newport, Tennessee

In 1960, the market moved to a larger building nearby, and the original building was remodeled for other businesses; that original building burned down in 1962. *Mary Gray.*

STUDIOS MOVED

Miss Mamie Campbell has this week moved her photographic studios from the Northcutt building on Church St. to the Allen building at the corner of Church and McMahan avenue. Miss Campbell will be glad to see all of her customers and friends at the new location in the corner next to the postoffice.

J. BUSHONG, TRAVELING PHOTOGRAPHER.

Pictures made in the best manner at prices to suit the times. Old Pictures Copied and Enlarged to any size with neatness and dispatch. The Beautiful Pearl Type also taken. Negatives preserved. Duplicates can be had at any time.

Pictures Good and Prices Low.

Now is your time before I go.

J. H. FAGALA PHOTOGRAPHER

Has recently opened a Gallery at his old Stand, in Newport, with new material and new outfit, and is now well prepared to execute all kinds of work in his line with promptness and to the satisfaction of every one, and at prices lower than ever known in Newport.

Pictures copied, enlarged or ensmalled Cash or Produce taken at market prices Call and examine my work

THIS PICTURE FINISHED BY
NINA'S PHOTO SHOPPE
NEWPORT, TENN.

KODAKS AND SUPPLIES

PROMPT RELIABLE FINISHING

SMITH DRUG COMPANY
The Rexall Store

FAST FILM DEVELOPING

Cameras   Portraits
Projectors   Weddings
Film   Frames
        Hallmark Cards

Painter's Photography

113 McMahan Avenue   Phone 623-7306

"Cocke County's Only Photographic Dealers"

Over the years, photography services were advertised in the local newspapers and school publications, as well as on the finished prints. *Author's collection.*

Education

'Tis education forms the common mind; Just as the twig is bent, the tree's inclined.
—Alexander Pope (1688–1744)

The need for education was recognized in young Newport. In 1806, just a few years after the county was formed, Anderson Academy was established. In 1813, community leaders participated in a state lottery that raised funds for the academy. Even though there was some public funding, this institution may have required tuition of its students, who were mostly well-to-do young males. The academy operated until the beginning of the Civil War.

Tennessee established a public school system in 1873. Irregular though it was, education was now available to all classes of society, male and female alike. Education for black children, unfortunately, was slower to develop.

When Newport (on the Big Pigeon River) began to develop, the first school was held in the Pisgah Presbyterian Church on the western edges of the settlement. When the Masonic Hall was finished in 1875, the Masons established a school, Newport Academy, on the ground floor. All classes were held here until Newport Grammar School was built in 1898 to serve both elementary and secondary students. Occasionally, enrollment at NGS was so large that some classes had to be held in the Masonic Hall. When Cocke County High School was built in 1917, Newport High School ceased to exist, and the entire building was used for elementary classes. Today, the original portion of Newport Grammar School is the oldest continually used elementary school in Tennessee. Additions to the facility were completed in 1924, 1950, 1961, 1966, 1982 and 2002.

There are both city and county school systems here, but in earlier times they were not as clearly defined as today. In 1906, R.P. Driskill was county school superintendent, but he taught secondary classes as Newport High School.

Before 1900, there was a school for black children, built somewhere on Jones Hill. In 1924, John M. Jones, a candidate for mayor, promised the black citizens a brick school. Despite some difficulties, this was accomplished, and Tanner Training School was established on Mulberry Street. This building was enlarged many times, although the original building has been razed. An interesting fact about Tanner was that the elementary classes were part of the city school system and the secondary classes were part of the county system. In 1965, school integration was initiated, and the next year Tanner was discontinued. The building is now called the Tanner Cultural System and houses several social service agencies.

Cocke County High School was a comprehensive facility offering both academic and vocational curricula. It was sometimes called "Central" because it was centrally located in the county. Always a county school, it has served the Newport students for more than ninety years. The original facility was used until 1963, when the school moved to the present campus.

Within the city limits were also Northport and West End, both county schools, which were consolidated into Northwest School in 1975.

Across the years, the schools of Newport have generated some outstanding results from all groups of students—male, female, black, white, rich and poor—all of whom recognized and profited from the opportunity that was available to them. Would that all students could be so insightful!

Pictures from the Past

Above: Cocke County High School (CCHS) home economics students Colleen Andrews, Sherry Moore and Robin Shropshire serve refreshments to school principal Joe Zavona, who headed the school from 1974 to 1987. *NPT photo.*

Right: Henry L. "Skip" Gregory served as principal both of Cocke County High School and Northwest School. His mother, Verta Gregory, was also a county principal. *NPT photo.*

Above: These CCHS band students represented the school at a regional band clinic in 1965. *From left*: Regenia Freeman, Denny Lankford, Brenda Bailey, Chuck Kisabeth and Danny Sluder. *NPT photo.*

Left: Wayne Waters served as principal of CCHS and superintendent of county schools. Here he is on the courthouse steps in 1939. *Tennessee Department of Forestry.*

Pictures from the Past

Meeting T.S. Gorman in Morristown in 1867, W.W. Langhorne (1841–1928) was told that the "new" Newport needed a teacher. Although Langhorne was an attorney, he accompanied Gorman back to the community and taught the first school here. Langhorne soon returned to his legal profession and practiced here until he moved to Washington state in 1890. *V.M. Phillips.*

H.G. Bray and Don Boley look over athletic trophies about 1962. Bray served as principal of CCHS, 1953–71. Boley left teaching for industrial work and then served several terms as Cocke County court clerk. *NPT photo.*

Pictures from the Past

"Julia, Virginia and Eva" are shown in 1933 in front of Newport Grammar School, which was established in 1898. *Chris Edmonds.*

Cocke County High School was opened in 1917. This building was used until 1963, when the school moved to the present campus. This picture was made before the gym was added in 1940. Baptist Convalescent Center now occupies the site. *Chris Edmonds.*

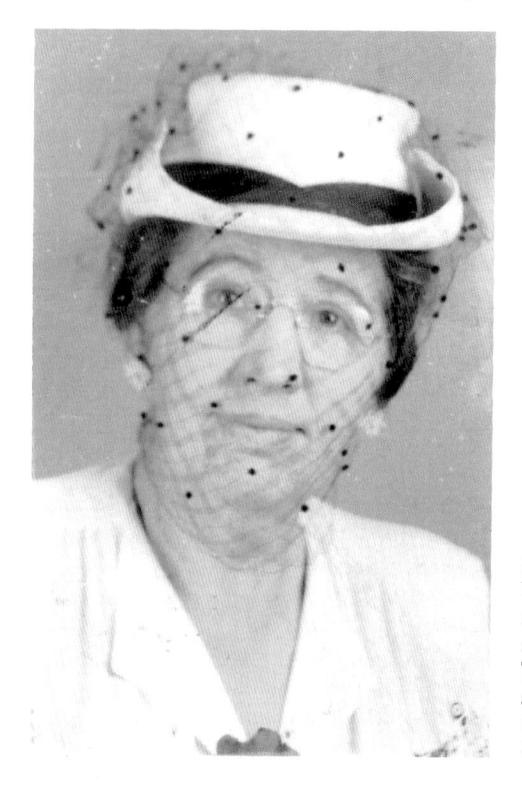

Known as "Lady Ruth," Mrs. Ruth Webb O'Dell (1886–1956) was a woman ahead of her time, serving as county school superintendent, president of East Tennessee Education Association and a state legislator, as well as authoring *Over the Misty Blue Hills: The Story of Cocke County, Tennessee. Author's collection.*

Lacy Wayne Vinson served as principal of Newport Grammar School and superintendent of the Newport City Schools, 1954–82. For all but two of those years, his wife, Theda, served as secretary and bookkeeper. *W.C. Vinson.*

Pictures from the Past

West End School opened in 1950 and operated until 1975. The building was razed in 2007. *SML Collection.*

A number of the faculty of CCHS in 1935 gathered in 1970 for a reunion of the class of 1935. *NPT photo.* *

Northport School opened in 1942 and was located on the hill above the intersection of Rhea and Lucia Streets. It closed in 1975. *Henry Gregory.*

Scenes

How dear to this heart are scenes of my childhood.
—Samuel Wadsworth (1784–1842)

Had you ever wished that you had a picture of some scene, structure or event that once was very important to you? If not, you at least know that it does not take long for scenes and buildings to change or disappear completely. Just traveling down a street can bring back memories of a building that once stood on a certain spot or a family who lived in a particular house.

To speak euphemistically, those of us who "have some age" can recall when certain local sites were just empty lots or fields or when some streets were not paved or did not even exist. Who can remember the one-lane bridge behind the depot or a downtown theatre?

Photographs can preserve those sights for the future. Just looking at old pictures proves that landscapes as well as persons can change. Photos actually made of persons can unexpectedly show something in the background that was at the time considered irrelevant. The capability of today's computer programs can accentuate these details.

When closing out his photography shop, Newport photographer Elza Painter regretted that over the years he had not taken more shots of local scenes and buildings, as much change had occurred since he went into business in 1959.

Remember, today's views are tomorrow's memories.

Newport, Tennessee

This and the two other sketches are the earliest known scenes of Newport and were published in a prospectus issued by the Newport Development Company in 1890. Looking west of Main Street, the first building is the Click House, now the police station. The next building was a home but is now Costner-Maloy Funeral Home. The Mims Hotel is next; it burned down in 1951. Beside it is the Mims Store. The city hall now occupies the site of the Mims buildings. The farthest building is the depot. *Author's collection.*

The courthouse in this picture was located on the same site as the present courthouse. The building in the foreground is located on the site of the First Christian Church. Manes Funeral Home occupies the site of the houses on the opposite side of the block. The artist was standing on the hill above the present library site. *Author's collection.*

Pictures from the Past

This view is looking south from across the river. The bridge in this picture was destroyed in the flood of 1902. Note the Masonic Hall on the hill. The church on the left is the Methodist Episcopal Church, South, and on the right is the Baptist church. *Author's collection.*

The new bridge in Newport in 1903. This one replaced the earlier one that went down in the 1902 flood. This bridge was used until 1957. The stones from the piers are now in the wall on Charles Rhyne Jr.'s lot on College Street. *Alexander Collection.*

Left: A later view of the mill dam shows much more water. *Chris Edmonds.*

Below: Another view of the bridge from about 1950. Older drivers will recall trying to access the bridge. *Author's collection.*

Pictures from the Past

The Burnett Bridge, just east of Newport. This bridge was used until the early 1970s. The home at the end of the bridge was occupied by the Barnes family. *Burnett Smith Collection.*

Main Street, looking east about 1955. The three buildings at the right burned down in 1973. The Park Theater was opened in 1938 and closed about 1955. *NPT photo.*

Main Street, looking west during a street repair project before 1920. *J.P. Masters.*

There was a swinging bridge over Big Pigeon River located very near the local history park. The remnants of the cables are still in the bluff. This picture was made about 1915. Dr. C.E. Barnett is the first man in the group. *Author's collection.*

Pictures from the Past

Main Street, looking from the Newport Mill about 1925. The little building in the foreground was used by the railroad crew. *Reba Williams.*

Certain places in Newport have always been prone to flooding after heavy rains due to the proximity to the river and wet weather springs. Jim Barnes is dealing with the problem here in May 1982. *NPT photo.*

Pictures from the Past

Part of this steel bridge over the French Broad River at Oldtown was washed away in the flood of July 1916. *NPT photo.*

Newport, Tennessee

This bridge was used until 1974 when the Dr. F.M. Valentine Sr. Bridge was opened. The river gauge is still standing. *Author's collection.*

There was once a gazebo located in the middle of Union Cemetery. Erected in 1905, it was removed in 1941. This picture was made in 1913. *SML Collection.*

Pictures from the Past

This is a view in 1960 from the present gym parking lot at Newport Grammar School. *NPT photo.*

This is Cosby Highway near I-40, looking toward the present site of McDonald's about 1975. *NPT photo.*

Newport, Tennessee

Election returns used to be posted on a board outside the *Newport Plain Talk* offices. This image was made about 1952. *NPT photo.*

The buildings are the same, but many of the businesses are different now in the Eastern Plaza Center. This picture is dated about 1975. *NPT photo.*

Transportation

*Travel, in the younger sort, is a part of education;
in the elder a part of experience.*
—*Francis Bacon (1561–1626)*

Transportation involves persons or goods moving or being moved from one place to another. On occasion, it has been necessary for persons to move, and such movements have affected history. Transportation, in fact, played a role in the origins of both old Newport and present-day Newport.

In 1799, it was decided (not without controversy) to establish the county seat of Cocke County on the French Broad River and name it "New Port," as the river was the principal transportation route at that time. Nearly seventy years later, local leaders debated whether the county seat should be on the Big Pigeon River, where the railroad, a more modern means of transportation, was located. Finally, the debate was settled, and "New Port" became "Newport."

Arriving here in 1867, the railroad right-of-way through what is now Newport was once the Gorman property. The Gorman brothers donated the land for the depot, and 140 years later, a depot is still on the site. At one time, the post office here was called "Gorman's Depot." For 60 years, the railroad was the means by which people and freight reached other destinations—even Morristown. Now, only freight passes through Newport, but at one time there were at least six daily passenger trains (three going west and three east). Chartered in 1900, the Tennessee and North Carolina Railroad was a smaller line and served the community.

Newport, Tennessee

The first automobile that came to Newport about 1909 had actually been ordered by someone who couldn't pay for it, so it was purchased by Dr. J.M. Masters. By 1915, a number of local citizens had automobiles, which necessitated the paving of city streets that had not really been suitable for travel. Even though there were still horses, buggies and wagons on the streets, the 1920s saw increasing sales of automobiles and a greater push for state and local governments to improve the roads. Bus service arrived here in the 1920s. The Dixie Highway (now 25/70) passed right through Newport and was a major route from Tennessee to North Carolina until Interstate 40 opened in October 1968. Ironically, passenger trains through Newport ended in December of that same year.

Transportation-related businesses such as automobile dealerships, parts stores, tire stores, repair shops, service stations, gasoline sales and car washes continue to be a major part of the local economy. Street maintenance is still a large part of the city budget.

Once relying on the rivers and the railroads to take them where they wanted to go, most Newport folks now have their own vehicles. They expect gasoline to be available, their rolling stock to be operable and the thoroughfares suitable for travel.

Pictures from the Past

A Tennessee Coach Line bus loads at the bus station, which was located at the corner of McSween and Broadway about 1950. *Author's collection.*

The Newport Kiwanis Club undertook a service project near Del Rio in 1922. The sign read: "Oh Boy! The Kiwanis Club of Newport made this place passable." *Author's collection.*

The Tennessee and North Carolina train about 1902. *Alexander Collection.*

Pictures from the Past

Right: A 1935 Mayflower is in front of the Plymouth agency of Joe Kyker. Later the building was the home of Cocke County Motor Company, which sold Fords. In 1974, the canopy was removed when John Porter converted the building into an office complex. *Author's collection.*

Below: The McNabb brothers' garage was located on the northeast corner of McMahan and Broadway, as in this 1915 photo. The building was originally the J.H. Susong Grain and Produce Warehouse. Later occupants were the A&P Store and the Firestone Store. The last occupant before the building was razed was Shoemaker's Florist. A portion of the Opera House can be seen at left. *McNabb Collection.*

Mayor George F. Smith is shown in front of Smith Drug Store in his car, which was the second one in Newport. *Chris Edmonds.*

A T&NC engine on the track near the Unaka Tannery. *Chris Edmonds.*

Pictures from the Past

After the T&NC locomotive ceased operations, residents along the line were served by the jitney, which made runs from Newport to Waterville. The box on the front reads "Newport Steam Laundry." Someone wanting to send a message to a person living along the line could tie a note to a rock, and the driver would toss out the rock when passing the receiver's home. *Chris Edmonds.*

The mechanics of Cocke County Motor Company posed in 1948. Kneeling is Garland Whitson. *Standing, from left*: Arvin Ledford, Everett "Pug" Palmer, Bartley Ledford and Arnie Carrell. *Author's collection.*

Newport, Tennessee

J. Lacy Myers began selling Chevrolets in Newport in 1927. He is shown here with a 1927 model in 1977 when he was honored for fifty years as a dealer. *NPT photo.*

Advertisements similar to this all over East Tennessee and Western North Carolina brought travelers to Art Fisher's garage in Newport, pictured in the background. Lola, Vaudalee, Donee and Lena Mae are shown with one of Art's mobile ads about 1930. *Jack Briggs.*

Pictures from the Past

The first hotel in Old Newport (log building at left). Was this where Debbie Milliken was licensed by the Court of Pleas and Quarter Sessions to keep a bar? *Chris Edmonds.*

Mims Hotel was located on the present Newport City Hall site. *Author's collection.*

Newport, Tennessee

Irish Cut Cabins were located on Highway 25/70, east of town. *Author's collection.*

T&S Service Station and Eureka Cabins were located just east of Fisher Bridge. *Author's collection.*

Pictures from the Past

Rhea Mims Hotel opened in 1925. It is now an NHA facility. *Chris Edmonds.*

Newport Motor Court and Newport Restaurant were located in west Newport on Highway 25/70. The site is now the Shamrock Apartments. *Chris Edmonds.*

Newport, Tennessee

Eisenhower Motor Court was adjacent to the Newport Motor Court. *Chris Edmonds.*

Tennessee Motor Court opened about 1967 on Cosby Highway (note the highway's narrowness). *Author's collection.*

Pictures from the Past

Holiday Inn opened in 1968 in conjunction with the opening of I-40. The name was changed to Mountain Crest Inn in 2009. *NPT photo.*

The Carolyn Motel was established by Mr. and Mrs. Artis Suggs and was named for their daughter, Carolyn Sue Cox. *Chris Edmonds.*

Newport, Tennessee

The Gorman brothers donated property for a depot on the line between their tracts. This depot was built by 1890 and fell prey to an arsonist in 1922. *Alexander Collection.*

Since passenger service to Newport ended in 1968, the present depot is now used by railroad maintenance crews. *Richard Remine.*

Civic Organizations

These new associations are composed of men and women of superior talents and sentiments…
—*Ralph Waldo Emerson (1803–1882)*

A civic organization is a voluntary group of citizens joined together with a shared goal in the hope of bettering their community in some way. Across time, these organizations have had a positive impact on Newport in such spheres as helping children and youth, the ill and disabled, the underprivileged and improvements to schools and government, as well as cultural, historical and personal development. Unlike earlier times, civic organizations are no longer rigidly separated by race and gender.

The oldest continually functioning civic organization in Newport is Lodge #234 of the Free and Accepted Masons, which actually predates the present town. First chartered in 1806, the lodge charter was later cancelled, only to be reinstated in 1866. The Masonic Hall, built in 1875, is the oldest building in town today. Coincidentally, the first women's organization on record was a group of forty-two local ladies who in 1874 pledged fifty cents each to provide desks for the new school being established by the Masons in their new building.

In the 1880s and 1890s, there were agricultural organizations such as the Farmers' Union and the Grange, several women's clubs, a theatrical troupe, a male social club and two veterans groups—the Grand Army of the Republic and the Confederate Veterans.

In addition to the Masons, the next oldest civic group here is the Kiwanis Club (1920), followed by the American Legion (1921) and the Business Women's Club (1924). A partial list of some of the other older organizations that are still active in Newport is found in the appendix.

Pictures from the Past

The Newport Red Cross has provided swimming lessons for local children for many years. Here, in 1974, Red Cross director Lucy J. Russell (seated) is overseeing the program's registration. The pool was later named in memory of Mrs. Russell. *NPT photo.*

Above: The Newport Garden Club was organized in 1938 and has hosted many flower shows, this one being for the iris, the Tennessee state flower. Club members shown are Marjorie Overholt, Ellen Moore and Frances Rhyne. *NPT photo.*

Left: The Twentieth Century Club was organized in 1914 and was once called the Mothers' Club. It built a clubhouse in 1964. Shown here are members Mary Louise Horton and Betty Jean Freeman, with packages to be sent to the military. The property now belongs to the First United Methodist Church. *NPT photo.*

Pictures from the Past

The Music Appreciation Club was organized in 1949. Inactive at present, a music scholarship is still given in memory of club founder Eleanor Little Hickey. *Author's collection.* *

The Easel Art Club was formed by the students of Dorothy P. Hauser, an artist who moved here in 1968. Shown here is one of its art shows at Parks Belk about 1972. *NPT photo.*

Pictures from the Past

A Boy Scouts organization was established here for a brief time in the 1920s. It was reorganized here in the late 1950s. In this 1968 photo, John Franklin Nelson has presented the tenderfoot rank to Ricky Freshour and Billy Naillon of Troop 297. *NPT photo.*

A group of Cub Scouts is pictured here with its leader, Nathan Inman, in 1974. *NPT photo.* *

109

The Appalachian Fair was organized here in 1904 but ceased in 1934. In 1949, the county fair was revived and continues today as the Cocke County Fair. Fair officials are meeting about 1965. *NPT photo.* *

Pictures from the Past

Fair officials attending a workshop in 1974. *NPT photo.* *

Above: A group gathered for the Veterans Day ceremony on the courthouse lawn in 1981. *NPT photo.* *

Left: The Newport Rescue Squad has been an active part of the community since its inception in 1959. One of its charter members was Newell "Hop" Byrd, who received an award from the Eastern Air Rescue Center. *NPT photo.*

Pictures from the Past

Organized in 1935, the Newport Music Club always worked for the advancement and understanding of good music in the community. *SML Collection.* *

The Beta Sigma Phi Sorority was chartered in 1949. The group is pictured here in 1954. *SML Collection.* *

Mary Lou Masters was crowned Beta Sigma Phi Girl of the Year in 1972. Standing with her are her husband, Jim Masters, and Mr. and Mrs. Fred Jones. *NPT photo.*

The Cocke County High School orchestra is shown here in 1939. *SML Collection.* *

Pictures from the Past

Sponsored by the Cosby Ruritan Club, the Cosby Ramp Festival has been a part of the local scene since 1954. This picture was made in 1960 at its original location, Shan-gri-la Hill, now the site of Stonebrook. *NPT photo.*

You are cordially invited to attend

The Dance
at the
Clifton Club

Newport, Tennessee, Wednesday, November, 2nd, 1921.

Dancing   The Pennsylvania
9:30 to 1:30   Serenaders

Present this card at the door

The Clifton Club, a social club for young Newport men, was organized in the late 1890s. It became inactive only to be revived for a few years after World War I. A group of young women adopted the name for an organization formed in 1939. *Author's collection.*

The Tennessee Picnic Association, organized in 1950, is a homecoming reunion for local black citizens and those who have moved to other parts of the country. The festivities are held every other year. *NPT photo.* *

Pictures from the Past

Honor guards composed by members of the local Veterans of Foreign Wars have willingly performed military funerals in the community. *NPT photo.* *

The honor guard organized by Clayton Bowman conducted a flag ceremony at First United Methodist Church in 1973. *NPT photo.* *

Pictures from the Past

Newport Lions Club was organized here in 1949. Shown about 1962, *from left*, are W.B. Haynes, Darius Miller, Zeno Wall (guest speaker) and Jim Masters. *NPT photo.*

Newport, Tennessee

The Rotary Club was organized here in 1958. Rotarians in this picture, *from left*, are John Hawk, Jack Hixon, Bill Fielding, Ralph Blackman and Frank Post. *NPT photo.*

A group of masters of the local Masonic Lodge are shown, with their years of service. *NPT photo.* *

Pictures from the Past

These men were launching the local United Way campaign in 1977: Mickey Thompson, Lonnie Jones, Don Jones, Tommy Smith, Ray Suttles, Johnny Hull and Jim McSween. *NPT photo.*

Newport, Tennessee

A festive event each summer was the Wagon Train, which began with a parade of horses and wagons through downtown and followed with a camp out. This picture is dated about 1967. *NPT photo.*

The Newport Kiwanis Club posed for this picture in 1966. *Don Jones.* *

Pictures from the Past

Shown is a group of the charter members of the Senior Citizens soon after being formally organized in 1973. The organization seeks to provide wider support services and opportunities for Newport's older residents. *NPT photo.* *

"Sertoma" is an acronym for "service to mankind." Locally, Sertoma was chartered in 1968. In this picture from about 1972 are David Long, Catherine Goodrum, Pat Osborne, Betty Britt and two unidentified people. *NPT photo.*

Religions

Religion is as healthy and normal as life itself.
—Charles Fletcher Dale (1845–1927)

An integral part of any community is its churches, which care for the spiritual life of the citizens. Since the first church came here in 1858, Newport has had congregations of many faiths.

The "mother church" of Cocke County is the Big Pigeon Baptist Church, which was organized in 1787. Though not in its original location, the church is still active on Mountain Ranch Road.

The Pisgah Presbyterian Church was established in Old Newport in 1832. The congregation changed locations in 1858 and erected a church adjacent to the Gorman Cemetery. This was the first church in present Newport. There it was used for Union Sunday School and then by both the Baptists and the Methodists for services, as well as being the first school. The building was demolished in the late 1930s, but the cemetery remains.

Organized in 1876, the Baptists erected their first church building on the present site in 1877. The Southern Methodists also had a church in Oldtown, but they erected their building here on the southeast corner of Mims Avenue and Broadway in 1885. Then the Northern Methodists built a church just up the street in 1892. In 1897, the Presbyterians moved from the western part of town and erected a new building nearby on McSween Avenue. The First Christian Church was built in 1928, so it is easy to see why Broadway once was called "Church Street."

Other churches, possibly forty or more and of various denominations, have been organized in all parts of the town, reinforcing the observation that no citizen is too far from the sound of a church bell.

Reverend Joseph Manning (1809–1888) was an early Baptist minister in the area. *Author's collection.*

Pictures from the Past

From an album dated 1902–3, this photo is captioned "old church in Oldtown." It is possibly the Pisgah Presbyterian Church, which moved to present Newport in 1858. *Alexander Collection.*

St. Agnes Catholic Church was located at the intersection of College Street and Woodlawn. Services ended here in 1943. *Author's collection.*

Good Shepherd Catholic Church was established in the Fred Fisher house. The Church of the Annunciation (Episcopal) also met for services here until the church purchased the former Andy's Restaurant in 1981. *Author's collection.*

As no photograph of the original building of First Baptist Church survives, Mrs. Robert Farmer did this painting based on the recollections of two of the older members, John Holder and Mrs. George Milne. This building was erected in 1877 and used until 1906. *Author's collection.*

Pictures from the Past

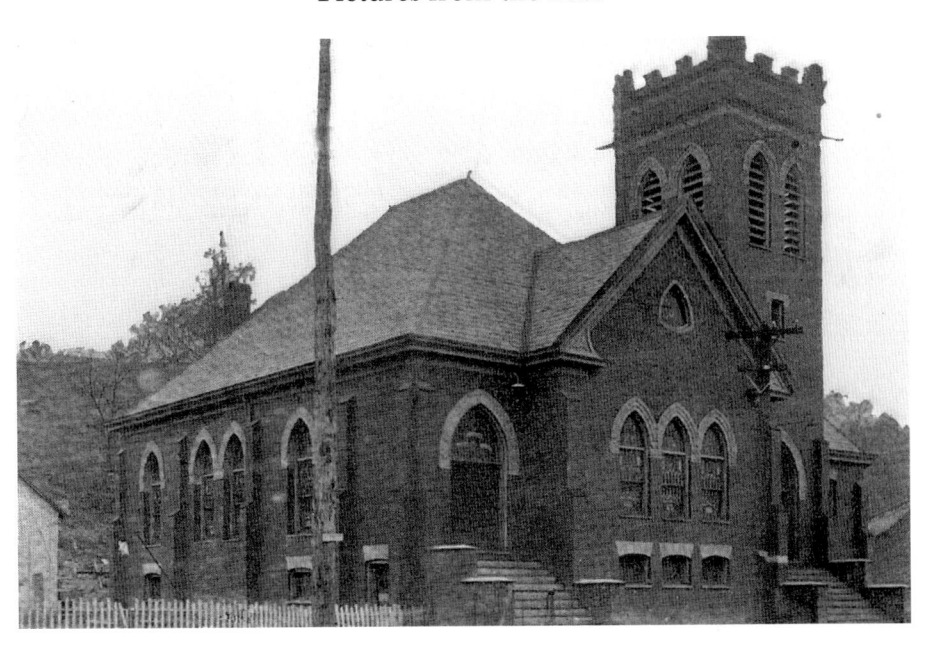

Above: This was the First Baptist Church from 1906 until the present building was built in 1955. This building was torn down in 1963 when the current educational wing was built. *Chris Edmonds.*

Right: In 1897, the Presbyterians built this church, which was used until 1969 when they moved to their new building on Hedrick Drive. The Newport Church of God then purchased this building and used much of the material, particularly the bricks and the windows, when building a new church on Woodson Road. *Chris Edmonds.*

> The pleasure of your presence is requested by the Ladies' Aid Society at their Thanksgiving Dinner, Presbyterian Church, Newport, Tennessee, Thursday, November 24, 1898, High noon.

No doubt the Presbyterian ladies were hosting the Thanksgiving dinner to help defray the costs of their new building. *Author's collection.*

Pictures from the Past

The Methodist Episcopal Church, South, was erected in 1909 following a fire that destroyed the congregation's earlier building on this site. This building was used after the two Methodist churches merged in 1941. It was razed after the new Methodist church was built in 1956–57. *Author's collection.*

Above: A group of local ministers gathered on Easter Sunday 1950 for the dedication of the new Methodist parsonage. *Author's collection.* *

Left: Dr. Harold Schulz, a former army chaplain, was pastor of the Holy Trinity Lutheran Church, 1966–72. *NPT photo.*

Pictures from the Past

The deacons of Macedonia Baptist Church are pictured at the dedication of their new church in 1978. *NPT photo.* *

Groundbreaking services occurred in 1976 for the Southside Baptist Church. *W.C. Vinson.**

The original New Zion AME Church on White Oak Avenue has been renovated and enlarged. *SML Collection.*

Pictures from the Past

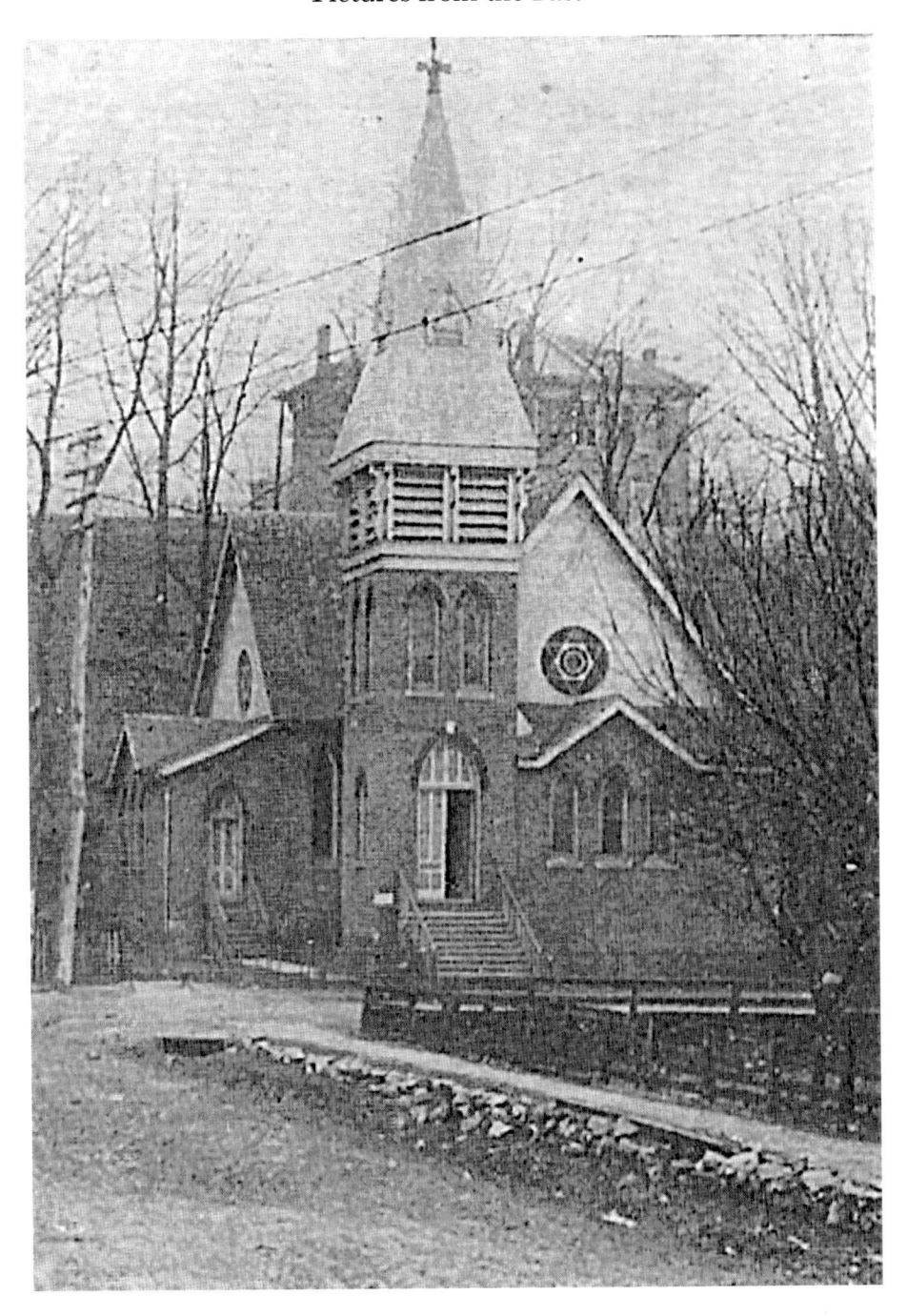

The Methodist Episcopal Church was built in 1892. When it was no longer used by the Methodists, this church was used by the Holy Trinity Lutheran congregation. It was razed in 1948. *Chris Edmonds.*

Newport, Tennessee

First Christian Church was organized in 1921 and has always occupied the northwest corner of Broadway and Baer Avenue. Its first building was erected in one day. The present church was built in 1928. *Arlene Hightower.*

A group of members of First Christian Church are gathered about 1953. *Arlene Hightower.* *

Recreation

Work first, then rest.
—*John Ruskin (1819–1900)*

The human body cannot work continuously; there must be some rest. God ordained that fact when a day of rest was set into the week. Just what constitutes rest and relaxation is truly an individual matter. History records various activities that offered diversion from the daily routine of work.

An early form of recreation was horse racing, and it is told that President Andrew Jackson, a lover of the sport, was here to attend a race on a track owned by General Alexander Smith. Mrs. Mims wrote about jousting tournaments, done on horseback, that were held here in 1883–87 and were reminiscent of medieval times. She said that, as she recollected, there were no ball teams here at that time.

An 1890 newspaper does mention a baseball team here, though. Beginning in 1937, and for several years after World War II, Newport had a semiprofessional baseball team called the "Canners." Little League teams were first organized here in 1953.

Football is another sport that gained popularity in the late 1800s. The first formally organized football team here may have been at Cocke County High School in 1916. One of the strong supporters of that first team was W.B. Stokely Sr., who had been on the first University of Tennessee "Big Orange" team in 1891. Little League football teams began here in 1962.

A golf course was developed here in 1926, but the Great Depression stifled its success. However, some of the golfers never lost their vision and later worked to establish the Smoky Mountain Country Club in 1957.

Newport, Tennessee

A Civil Works Administration project, the Newport City Park, was created in 1936 on the old Appalachian Fairgrounds. Over the years, it has provided the citizens a place to enjoy swimming, tennis, basketball, football, baseball, exercising and picnicking.

Fishing and hunting, once necessary to put food on the table, have evolved into popular recreational activities. With the completion of Douglas Lake in 1943, boating has also become popular.

The fine arts—music, drama and painting—have brought relaxation to citizens here over the years.

Again, what is relaxing varies from person to person and from time to time. Teenagers in Newport today would probably not be as excited as the graduating class of Newport High School was in 1912 when they were entertained by John and Claudia Holder with "automobile rides around the town."

The Newport City Park pool has been enjoyed by innumerable citizens both young and old since it first opened in 1937. The green shingled pavilion housed the dressing rooms and the snack bar. It was razed to build the current pavilion. *NPT photo.*

Pictures from the Past

Mrs. Ann Ruble from the Employment Security office meets with the summer City Park pool crew in 1971. *NPT photo.* *

Newport, Tennessee

Above: There was a racetrack, located at the old Appalachian Fairgrounds, used for horses, motorcycles and stock cars. Part of the racetrack, later converted to the driveway through the park, is still recognizable. This motorcycle race was dated about 1928. *Author's collection.*

Left: Cleo Giles's stock car would have been racing at the fairground track in the early 1930s. *Chris Edmonds.*

Pictures from the Past

Bowling has been in Newport since the 1930s. One set of lanes opened in 1951, and then Victory Lanes opened in 1961. The bowlers posed with their trophies about 1962. *NPT photo.* *

The lady bowlers were known as "the BB's" and were sponsored by Mohawk Mills. *NPT photo.* *

The Smoky Mountain Country Club opened in 1958. A group of golfers posed about 1962. *NPT photo.* *

Pictures from the Past

Red Gardner (right), the golf course pro, awarded trophies to Jack "Catfish" Sams and David Whaley in 1972. *NPT photo.*

Tennis was also once offered at Smoky Mountain Country Club. This picture is dated 1979. *NPT photo.* *

Pictures from the Past

Never one to miss a financial opportunity, Art Fisher turned his garage into a boxing arena in 1929. Notice the fish that was always a part of his advertisements. *Carol Urban.*

Popular singing and television star Tennessee Ernie Ford was the featured celebrity at the Ramp Festival in 1959. Ford is talking with Fred Myers and Governor Buford Ellington. To the right of Ford are his mother Mrs. C.T. Ford, Mrs. L.S. Nease and Rella Ruth Rader. Standing in the rear are Martha Walker and Clyde Hodge. *Author's collection.*

Pictures from the Past

Above: Doris Mims, probably dressed up for the big parade on July 4, 1913. It is unfortunate that the identity of the young Uncle Sam is unknown. *Roadman Collection*.

Right: Two young Newport swains, Bill Jones (left) and Burnett Smith, casually dressed. The photo, captioned "seeking flowers on other mountains," is dated about 1913. From the other photos in the album, apparently it was female "flowers" they sought. *Burnett Smith Collection*.

This group was about to depart on an excursion to Crestmont via train on June 29, 1912, in honor of newlyweds Fain and Mary (Snoddy) Smith, who are pictured in the center of the group. *Burnett Smith Collection.* *

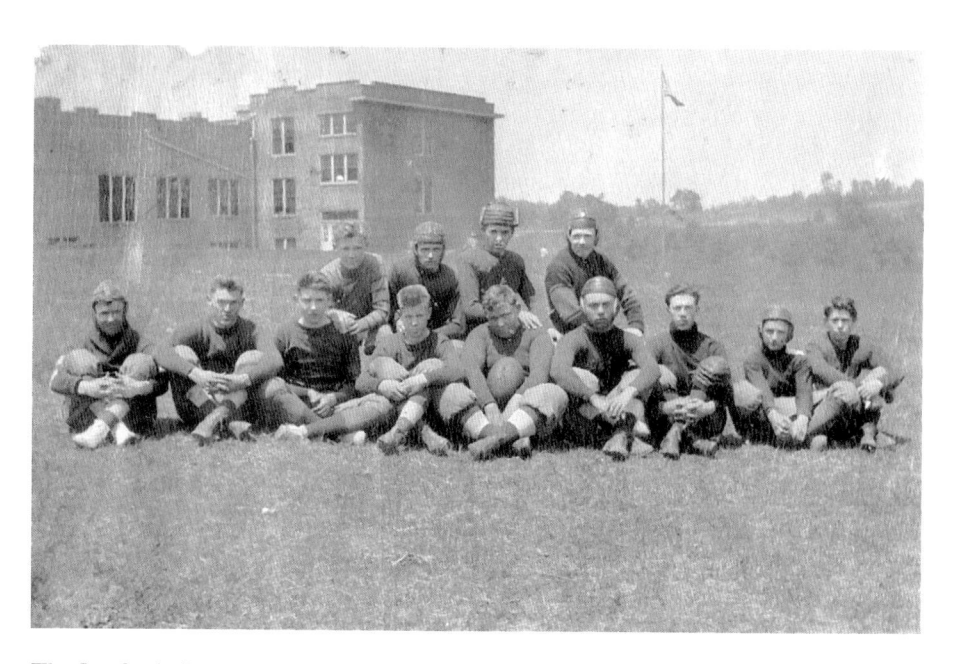

The first football team at CCHS in 1917 is pictured here, with the school in the background. *Evan Smith Collection.* *

Pictures from the Past

This is the girls' basketball team at CCHS in 1919. *Evan Smith Collection.* *

In 1919, the boys' basketball team was practicing in the school gymnasium, which was later used as the cafeteria. *Evan Smith Collection.*

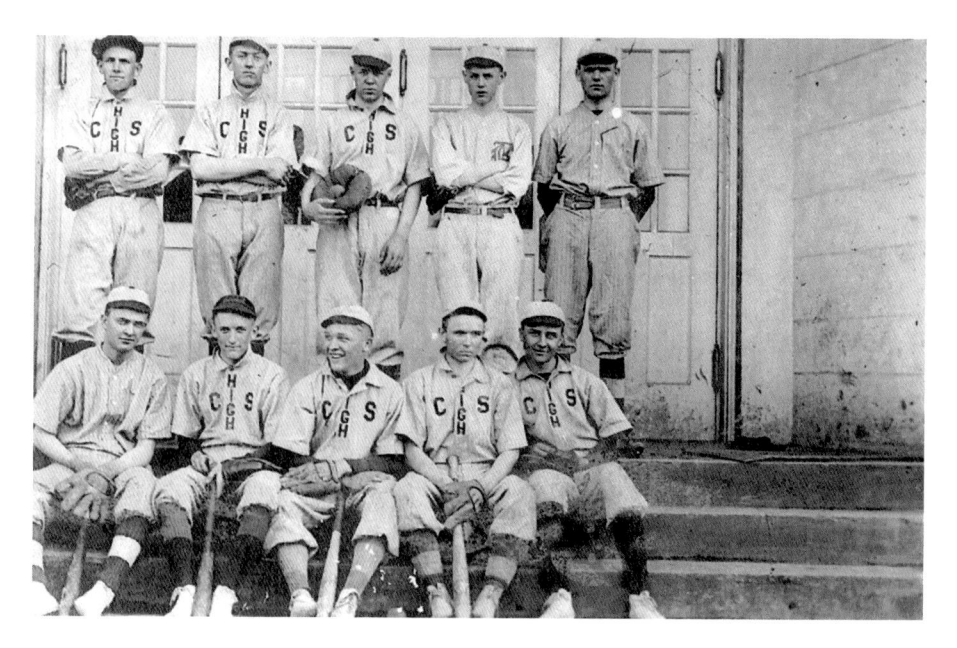

The baseball team at CCHS posed on the front steps of the school. *Evan Smith Collection.* *

Pictures from the Past

These girls composed the basketball team in 1912 at the old Newport High School. *From left*: Alma Ailey, Arlie Burke, Edna Sparks, Lucy Boyer and Edith Balch. *Burnett Smith Collection.*

Baseball player Steve McNabb is being handed a ball by Harry Melton about 1962 at the Newport City Park. Others in the group include an unidentified man, Bob Kilpatrick, Royce McNabb, Bill Lewis and Walter Shell Jr. *NPT photo*.

Early Newport residents often sought relief from the summer heat at Carson Springs, at the foot of English Mountain. This springhouse, replacing an earlier one, was destroyed by fire in the early 1970s. Today the spring itself is almost covered by debris. *Author's collection.*

Appendix
Group Photograph Identifications

Citizens

Page 14: *Seated, from left*: Jehu T. Stokely, Edith Estes Stokely, Anna Rorex Stokely, Fannie Stokely Fisher, James R. Stokely and Amelia Graham Stokely. *Standing, from left*: George Stokely, Carrie Lou Stokely, John M. Stokely, Anna Mae Stokely and William B. Stokely.

Page 15, top: Seated, at top, are Philip and Mariah (Feight) Fisher. Standing between them is Ola Fisher White. On the bottom step are Arthur Jackson Fisher, John W. Fisher and A. Newton Fisher. In the middle row are Nannie Dennis Fisher, Jesse A. Fisher and J. Cambridge Fisher.

Page 17, top: Top is Sarah Margery Murphy O'Brien; next is her daughter Margaret O'Brien McNabb, followed by grandson James Ruby McNabb and great-grandson.

Page 18, top: *Standing, from left*: Reece Balch, Gerald Jenkins, Ronnie Buckner, Dennis Webb, John Parker, Arvine Taylor, Ralph Wade Giles and Jim Lethco.

Page 34, bottom: *Seated, from left*: Mayor Fred M. Valentine Jr. and Aldermen James P. Masters, Harry Melton, Ray Proffitt, James H. Burnett Jr. and Neil Rader. *Standing, from left*: City Attorney Roy T. Campbell Jr., Judge George R. Shepherd and City Recorder Bill Whitson.

Appendix

Business/Industry

Page 51, bottom: *Standing, from left*: Maurice M. Roberts, Nancy Bryant, Dean Moore, Kathy Smith, Peggy Chrisman, Kathleen Massey, Ann Smith, Sandra Crum, Imogene Webb, F. Nolen McCoig and W.G. Ottinger.

Page 55, top: *Standing, from left*: Doyle Barger, Assistant Manager Jack Hawk, Michael Hayworth, Mr. and Mrs. Charles Cobble and Betty Carver.

Page 58, bottom: *Seated, from left*: W.A. Roberts, Aaron O'Dell, Frankie Mae Hixson, Neil Harper and Ralph Jones. *Standing, from left*: Burl Roberts, Glenmore Smith, Carl Gilland, Hugh Roberts, Kenneth Kite, Ned Lovell, Margaret Miller, Dewey Webb, Herbert Hurst, Reva Dean Bryant, Mack Olden, Charles Gray, Harold Hurst, Paul O'Dell and Paul Penland.

Page 60, top: *Seated, from left*: Librarian Pauline Walker, Joann Etherton, Katie Coffey (Area Resource Center) and Board Chairman Patsy Williams. *Standing, from left*: Ralph Blackman (Heywood-Wakefield), unidentified, M.L. Bowers (Newport Utilities), Charles Rhyne Jr. (Rhyne Lumber Company), Fred Mobley (Firestone), Don Foust (Electro-Voice), E.H. Kennedy (Stokely's), Bill Williams (Rhyne Lumber Company), Jim Ethier (Bush Brothers) and Jim Stout (Wood Products).

Page 61, top: Human Services employees standing, *from left*, are Martha Walker, Loiree Grigsby, Nancy Watts, Harold Cates, Emma Griffin and Martha Laws.

Page 62, bottom: National Bank of Tennessee officials, *seated*, are Cashier George B. Nye, President Charles T. Rhyne and Ben Ray. *Standing, from left*: Herbert S. Walters, William Spradlin, Curtis Allen, J. Donald Cody, Fred L. Myers Sr., Dr. Fred Valentine Sr. and Clyde Driskill Sr.

Education

Page 75, bottom: Teachers (1935), *standing, front*, are Marjorie McMahan, Doris M. Parrott, Lagretta C. Parrott and Sue S. Kennedy. *Rear*: Comer Johnson, Perle S. Cody, Paul McRee, Luzelle S. Babb, Estalena W. Murrell and E.H. "Buzz" Kennedy.

Group Photograph Identifications

Civic Organizations

Partial list of Newport civic organizations: American Legion Auxiliary, Business Women's Club, Cancer Society, Newport Chamber of Commerce, Choral Club, Crewettes, Democrats, Eastern Star, Epsilon Sigma Alpha, Farm Bureau, Heart Fund, Heartease Garden Club, Hilltopper Club, Home Demonstration Clubs, Household of Ruth, Jaycees/Jaycettes, Junior Order, March of Dimes, Medical Society, Ministerial Society, Modern Woodman, Optimists, Odd Fellows, Parent-Teacher Association, Retired Teachers, Serio-Sabio Club, Sesame Circle, Tenasee Club, Tuberculosis Society, Theater Guild, United Daughters of the Confederacy, Veterans of Foreign Wars, Winookski Circle and Women's Christian Temperance Union.

Page 107: Music Appreciation Club members in 1974, *from left*, are Eddie Walker, Juanita Gay, Eleanor Hickey, Mary Ann Little, Beth Hogan, Marie Selser, Elizabeth Thomas, Hugh William Hightower, Arlene Hightower and I.M. Selser.

Page 109, bottom: Cub Scouts, *front row*, are Wesley Ellison, Clay Henderson, Dave Henderson, Clyde Allen and Mickey Harper. *Back row*: Mark Parrott, Scott Green, Mark Ford, Doug Mooneyham and Tyler Grooms.

Page 110: Fair officials, *from left*, are County Agent Hugh Russell, Allen Thomas, Virginia Cureton, Mary Louise Horton, Charlene Hawk and Ike Dawson.

Page 111: Fair officials, *from left*, are Pearl Ragan, Louise Shoun, Mary Hurst, Ruth Crum, Maude O'Neil, Shirley and David Ottinger and County Agent Ray Stockdale.

Page 112, top: Presenting flag to Sheriff Bobby Stinson are Nancy L. O'Neil and Mary L. Nodell from the Daughters of the American Revolution. *Standing, rear, from left*: Cecil Samples, Herb Harper, Veteran Service Officer Dutch Mason, Wallace Sutton and trumpeters Tommy Puckett and Steve Tweed.

Page 113, top: Music Club officers (1956–57) were Mrs. John C. Holder, Mrs. F.M. Mason, Mrs. Houston Seehorn, Mrs. James Burnett, Mrs. P.T. Bauman (sponsor), Miss Mazie Knight, Mrs. Lee Freeman, Mrs. Earl Rhodes and Mrs. Alex Fancher.

Appendix

Page 113, bottom: Beta Sigma Phi members, *seated*, are Suella Ottinger, Betsy Bible, Elsie Siskin, Christine Gorman, Myra Hartsell and Norma Jean Huffman. *Standing, from left*: Rozelle Holt, Edith Thompson, Lois Reese, Eva Gaddis, Marjorie Balch, Mazie Knight, Melba Bailey, Elizabeth Jones (sponsor), Helen Templin, Wilma Penland, Eunice McDonald, Dorothy Gray, Carolyn Sue Cox, Jamie Freshour and Georgia Overholt.

Page 114, bottom: Orchestra members, *front row*, are Anne Ellison, Jeanne Carmichael, Dorothy Ann Doak, Sarah Eva Susong, Viola Chaney and Charles Rhyne Jr. *Middle row*: Charles Ernest Ottinger, Pete Hambaugh, Alf Swann, Edward Walker and Buddy Nelson. *Back row*: Douglas Amick, Mrs. P.T. Bauman (director) and Evan Fisher.

Page 116: *From left*: Newport mayor Rolan Dykes, State Historian Wilma Dykeman Stokely, unidentified, Cynthia Finch, Bessie Thomas and Dave Hayworth.

Page 117: Veterans of Foreign Wars Honor Guard, *from left*, are Hence Hayes, Campbell Evans, Fred Murr, Bill Cogdill, C.C. Brown, Billy Jack Martin, Herb Harper, Charles Sweeten, Venus Williamson, Charles Murr and Jack Holt.

Page 118: Honor Guard members at First United Methodist Church, *from left*, are L.S. McKay, Troy Stuart, Clayton Bowman, Billy Parks, Lee O. Boye, J.B. Conard, William Keller, Bill Vasquez, Raymond Sutton, Ron Smith and Buddy Greene.

Page 120, bottom: Master Masons, *from left*, are Robert Kisabeth, Rowe Parks, Orville Stephenson, J.O. McCurry, Joe Dick Moore, Glenmore Smith and Tom J. Stokely.

Page 122, bottom: *First row*: Elza Painter, Dr. W.B. Henry, Tip Brown, Jim Runnion, Niles Kitchen, A.L. Petrey, Creel Helms, M.L. Bowers Jr. and Carolyn Kickliter (pianist). *Second row*: John Abe Teague, Jim Stout, Hugh Russell, J. Kenneth Porter, Troy Crawford, Hoyle Ratcliff, Floyd Williams and W. Glenn Ottinger. *Third row*: Clyde Driskill Sr., Dr. D.C. Amick, Vaughn Lewis Moore, John Holder, Don Foust, J. Donald Cody, Bill G. Williams and James H. Burnett Jr. *Fourth row*: Dr. J.A. Hardin, James C. McSween, Dean Williams, J. Lacy Myers, Eddie Sklar, Dr. Craig Ratliff, Dwight Wilkerson,

Group Photograph Identifications

H.C. Roberts and Bob Smith. *Fifth row*: Reid Bailey, Bill Eldridge, Ken Newman, Russell King, Charles S. Runnion, Dr. Fred Valentine Sr., Ben W. Hooper, Howard Gandy and Earl Rhodes. *Sixth row*: A.A. Lamons, C.D. Fisher, Gordon Williams, Bob Kilpatrick, Ben D. Stokely, Everett Freshour, Wade Allen, Charles Kickliter, Joe Kyker Jr. and Maurice Suggs.

Page 123: Senior Citizen members identified in this group include Mary Rowland, Nora Clevenger, Grace Lindsey, Nina Campbell, Sally Butler, Burnett Vinson, Ruth Crum, Ida Gaddis, Mack Suggs, T.J. Crum, Dan Ragan and Larmie Butler. Sadly, many are unidentified.

RELIGIONS

Page 132, top: Ministers at the Methodist parsonage dedication, *from left*, are Dan Bowers (Newport Presbyterian), Reverend Luke Linebarger (Holy Trinity Lutheran), Dr. Carl P. Daw (First Baptist), Methodist Bishop Paul Kern, Reverend Harrell Russell (First Methodist) and District Superintendent Reverend W.H. Harrison.

Page 133: *In front*: James Goodrum and Roland Dykes. *In rear*: Joe Carr, Virgil Dirl, Reverend C.J. Mize, Jerry Goodrum, Billy Davis and Fox Knox.

Page 134, top: At Southside groundbreaking, *from left*, are Dr. Duane Conner (First Baptist Church), Joe Kyker, Charles Creasy, Johnny Carson, Roy Proffitt, Conn Murrell, Mrs. Ivan Babb, W.C. Vinson and Richard Williams.

Page 136, bottom: *First row*: Sally Vassar, Gertrude Maddron, Coralyn Hightower, Linda Evans, Glenda Dean Ealy, unidentified, Oscar Paul Gregg, Donnie Shell, unidentified, Bud Carver and Bill Finchum. *Second row*: Bibert Kyker, Delia Raines, Helen Carver, Polly Ealy, Adalyn Justus, Patsy Thornton, Mollie Cline, Allene Gray, Ednora Gregg, Anna Jean Shell, Laura Craddock, Betty Sweeten and Dr. Fred Craddock. *Third row*: Belva Maddron, Mary Rowland, Ruby Jones, Bonnie Lindsey, Beatrice Ottinger, Elizabeth Justus, Addie Evans, Dean Ealy, Beulah Sweeten, W.M. Crowe, Howard Justus, Sam Raines, Edna Thornton, Oscar Gregg, Fred Mann, Lucy Shults, Elizabeth Woodson and Oth Maddron.

Appendix

Recreation

Page 139: Mrs. Ann Ruble is on the far right. *Front, from left*: Delores Jones, Eutha Louise Proffitt and Rubye Maddron. *Back, from left*: Larry Brown, Butch Williams, Terry Fancher and Mickey Powers.

Page 141: Kneeling are Bob McCoy and George "Gump" Lewis. *Standing, from left*: Ned Lovell, M.E. Edwards, Roy Yater, Jim Burnett and Clarence Sams.

Page 142, top: Seated are Sue Hartsell and Peggy Jones. *Standing, from left*: Lois Sluder, Charlotte Cureton, Wilma Williams and Irene Lampson.

Page 142, bottom: Kneeling are Homer Henry, Johnny Jones, Danny Walchack, James Burchette and Fred Lesley. *Standing, from left*: L.D. Brooks, unidentified, Bill Henry, Ned Lovell and Bob McCoy.

Page 144: *Seated, from left*: Kay Verble, Pam Graham, Pat Shults and Kathy Ethier. *Standing, from left*: Butch Martin, Gary Verble, Roger Catron, Terry Hurst and Jim Ethier.

Page 148, top: Although the entire group is not in the picture, those listed as going on the excursion were Mr. and Mrs, Fain Smith, Reverend J.S. Black, Mrs. Rhea Minnis, Mrs. W.D. McSween, Misses Ethel Snoddy, Nell Kidwell, Madge Mims, Annie White, Bonnie Bell, Bert Samones, John Ruble, Henry Alexander, C.E. Barnett, Burnett Smith, Carl McNabb, Lee Smith and Carl Mims.

Page 148, bottom: *Seated, from left*: Oliver Gray, James McSween, William Stokely, Tom Warren, Orton Delozier, Ordway Delozier, Charles McSween, Herbert Murray and Lone Sisk. *Standing, from left*: Clyde Driskill, Evan Smith, Ward Goughnour and Joe Dawson.

Page 149, top: *From left*: Anna B. Hooper, Margaret Smith, Jennie Boyer, Trilby Jones, Miss Drinkard (coach), Lois Hixon, Pearl Johnson, Anna Stokely and Mabel Sparks.

Page 150: Members of the team are Robert Hickey, Fred Valentine, Tom Warren, John Balch, Sam Holt, Beecher Bridges, Oliver Gray, Burnett Boyer, Sanford Jack, Wiley Kirk and Ruby Ford.

About the Author

Edward Walker is a native East Tennessean who has been interested in local history since his high school days. His working career has been that of a teacher mostly in secondary social studies. He has compiled and published several books on historical and genealogical topics. He lives in Newport, Tennessee, with his wife and daughter.

Visit us at
www.historypress.net